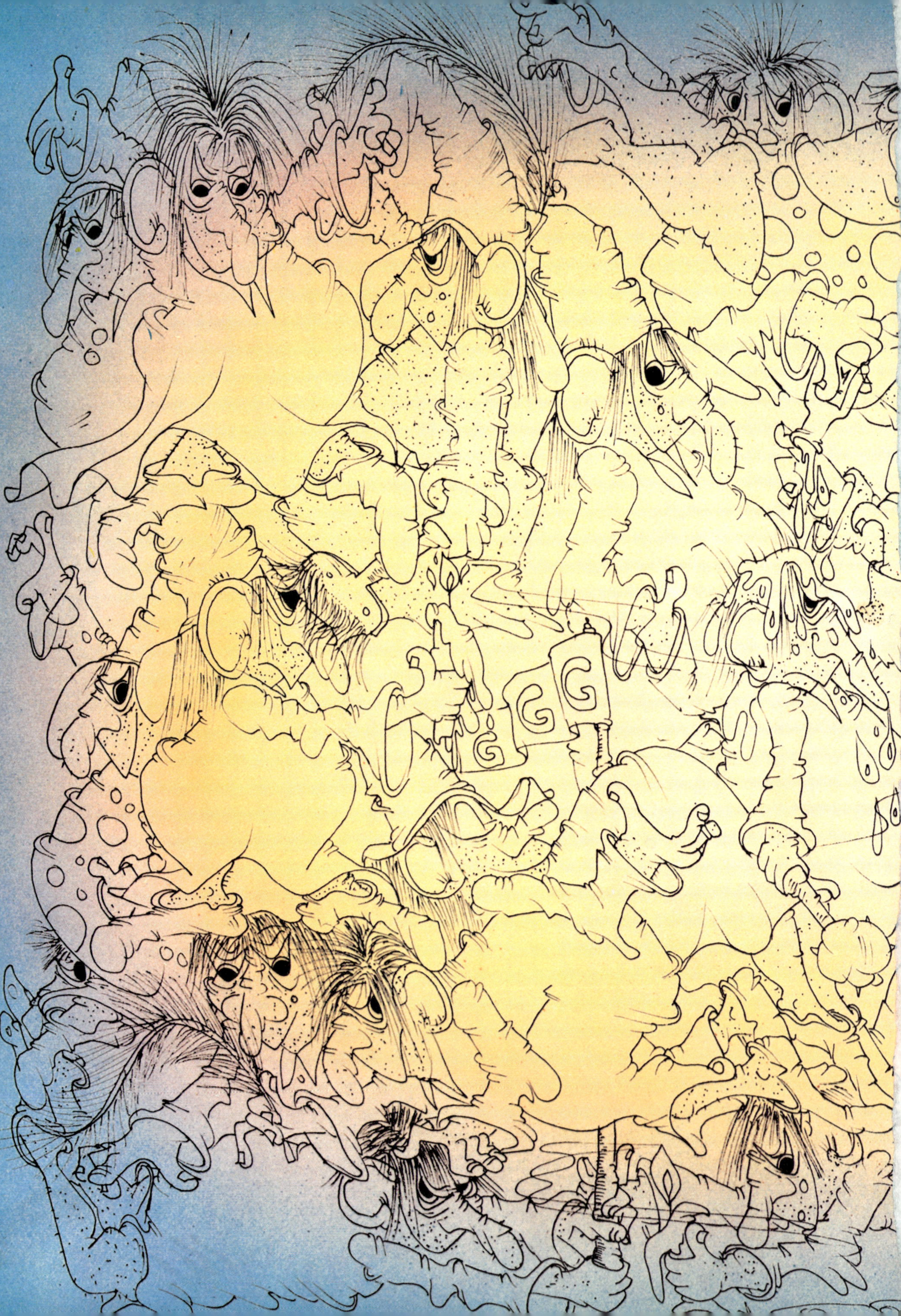
G G G

THE BOOK OF GREMLINS

MICHAEL RIDLEY
and
BRYAN NEARY

J.M. DENT and SONS LTD.
London · Toronto · Melbourne

First published in Great Britain
in 1980 by J.M. Dent and Sons Ltd.
Aldine House, Welbeck Street, London.

Printed and bound
in Hong Kong
by Toppan
Printing Co., Ltd.

To
KIRAN
JOSEPH
and
SAMANTHA

ISBN 0 046 04500 8

This book was
designed, edited and produced by
Origination
73 Warnford Road, Bournemouth,
Dorset, Great Britain.

Handwriting by
Jackie Ridley.

Contents

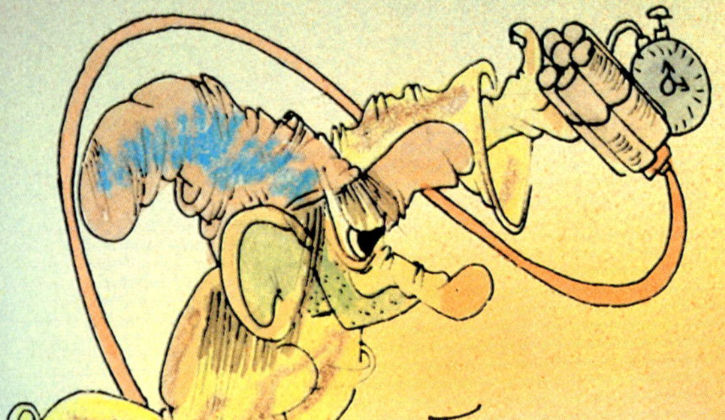

WHAT ARE GREMLINS ?

This book is the result of many years of painstaking research and investigation into Gremlins. We have observed them in many lands, both in their natural habitat, i.e. in peoples' homes, places of work and leisure, as well as in the laboratory. This field work has proved invaluable when piecing together a picture of their life styles and social behaviour. Careful questioning of a number of specimens has led to the discovery of an international control centre for Gremlins, as well as the until now top-secret Gremlin code. Through an unexpected stroke of luck, we have been able to penetrate Gremlin Control and see for ourselves how Gremlins are organized and governed and how every mission or task is carefully planned.

But before we can reveal all this to our readers, perhaps we should pause and ask, just what is a Gremlin? Well, according to the Oxford English Dictionary it is :- "A mischievous sprite alleged to cause mishap to machinery, etc.". It goes on to say that the Gremlin is a 20th century phenomenon, but says its origin is unknown.

Webster's Dictionary, on the other hand defines a Gremlin as :- "A small gnome, held to be responsible for malfunctions of equipment, especially in an aeroplane".

There are two points in these definitions that we can now show to be incorrect. The first is that Gremlins are not gnomes—for our research indicates that they are in no way related. To mistake Gremlins for gnomes is a common error. For it seems that any little mythological creature is called a gnome, a goblin, a fairy or, in Ireland, a Leprechaun.

Gremlins, however, are quite distinct, their only similarity being their size and even this we have found to be variable, depending upon the job they have been allocated by Gremlin Control. Some observers have suggested that the name Gremlin is, in fact, derived from goblin, but our findings indicate that this is highly unlikely.

The second point is that Gremlins are a 20th century phenomenon. This is far from the truth—for our studies behind the dusty shelves of libraries and through the debris of human history, quite clearly show that Gremlins have existed as long as humans. Mankind has always been aware of their presence and has called them by many names.

What is true, however, is that Gremlins have only been a major force in human affairs since the Industrial Revolution and the introduction of wide-spread mechanization. In this respect they are indeed a modern malady.

The name Gremlin came into prominence early this century with aviators who attributed the innumerable faults of their flying-machines to Gremlins. They believed there were Gremlins for just about everything........ how right they were.

Through painstaking research into the wreckage of major and minor disasters of history and of modern times (much of it our own) we have been able to piece together a complete dossier on Gremlins and can now present these facts to the public for the first time.

As normally Gremlins cannot be seen, we had to develop the gremelscope which, although a somewhat primitive instrument, enabled us to observe them. We had hoped to present the results of our research with photographs, but our experiments at photographing the creatures proved quite disastrous. They simply would not register on existing film. We then developed gremelchrome, but even though we achieved an image, the results were not good enough for reproduction.

We therefore had no alternative but to concentrate on the development of the gremelscope, and eventually perfected not only an advanced laboratory model, but also a portable, easily wearable version, which we used for field work.

We have therefore presented our results within these pages with highly accurate pictorial representations, drawn from life by Bryan Neary (known to Gremlins as Bryzee) who has used the gremelscope to great effect.

After just a short time of using the gremelscope we noticed that there are not as many female Gremlins as males. This at first puzzled us as we couldn't understand how Gremlins could exist

in such large numbers without a fairly equal population. It was only after many months of observation, following up numerous cases of gremlinfestation, that we made our first big discovery. Gremlins are unlike any other mythological creatures, for they do not reproduce themselves. They are mind creatures, born out of human desires, aspirations and emotions. Thus they are created by humans themselves! Another surprising discovery has been that once created they do not die - thus Gremlins can be many hundreds of years old.

Most of the strange, amazing and inexplicable happenings to mankind can be explained by gremlinfestation. Although their actions seem disastrous from the human point of view, we have evidence to show that they are not necessarily hostile. Thus, good and bad happenings may be ascribed to Gremlin activity. Nevertheless they have had a profound effect on human progress.

GREMLIN ♂
Gremlinus allegorica

Order: MYTHOLOGICA
Family: IMAGINARAE

This is the first scientific illustration of a Gremlin (magnification 400x)

The specimen shown is a fully grown male, aged about 500 years. He is wearing standard Gremlin clothing (regulation issue).

It was particularly difficult to persuade him to stay in front of our laboratory gremelscope long enough to draw him accurately and it was only after being bribed with the promise of a successful grem,* that he agreed to co-operate.

*The word commonly used by Gremlins to describe the act of aggravating a human. As we will show, grems can cause minor irritation or major havoc, depending on the status of the Gremlin.

GREMLIN ♀
Gremlinus domestica

Order : MYTHOLOGICA
Family : IMAGINARAE

The female Gremlin, otherwise known as a gremlina * is very rarely seen, for she is normally gremeated ϕ by female emotions and desires. As the human female has generally been more passive than the human male, the numbers of female Gremlins was not large. However, with the emancipation of women and the growth of women's lib, female Gremlins have increased dramatically. It is expected that there will be equal numbers of male and female Gremlins by the end of the 1980's.

* "Gremlin" usually refers to both sexes.
ϕ Gremlinese verb for the creation of a Gremlin.

GREMLIN
Gremlinus allegorica
Infant ♂

Another surprising fact that we discovered in the course of our field observation of Gremlins, is that they go through babyhood and childhood. We at first found this odd, as we knew that Gremlins are mind creatures and had thus expected them to be gremeated fully grown. It seems, however, that they first appear in infantile form and progress rapidly to the adult stage, the time taken depending on their function. Both male and female infants are fully operational and can carry out successful grems in whatever form they take, although usually under the direction and guidance of adult Gremlins.

The illustration on the left shows two studies of the infantile form of G380 (all Gremlins have serial numbers), a specialist in the ancient art of angling. Izaak Walton mentioned him in his classic work "The Compleat Angler". We include a sketch of him in adult form in "A Guide to Gremlin Spotting", later in the book.

The little gremlina* shown on this page is slightly older than the boy on the left. She is playing with a gremonster^Φ.

TECHNICAL NOTE: The gremelscope was set to a magnification of 800x to achieve this clarity.

* Name for a female Gremlin.

Φ An indecisive human emotion which manifests itself as a mini-monster — of no threat to humans, but which young Gremlins love to play with. They eventually fade away.

GREMLIN
Gremlinus allegorica
Infant ♀

GREMLIN FAMILY GROUP

Frontal View

Gremlins are anthropoid creatures, resembling humans in many respects. It is impossible to state their size as it varies according to the grems they undertake. As a general rule they are extremely small, especially those that work in fine mechanisms like watches, clocks, computers etc.

A Gremlin has the capacity of altering his size at will. Some physical characteristics and proportions are exaggerated.

In appearance they take on the racial characteristics of the area in which they work or were gremeated. They do not need food or drink to sustain them, but they do need sleep — in fact some Gremlins are quite addicted to it!

GREMLIN FAMILY GROUP

Posterior or Cheeky View

GREMADOG

Canis gremlinsis

Order: CARNIVORA
Family: CANIDAE

Perhaps one of the strangest facts we discovered about Gremlins is that, like humans, they have canine companions. The Gremadog is similar to the Gremlin in origin – it too is a mind creature, created not from human emotions and aspirations, but from those of the dog, a creature that has lived with man for thousands of years. Apart from being a Gremlin's best friend, Gremadogs also grem- but cause only random havoc of a non-specialist kind.

The specimen shown here is Champion Snarlingfang of Inbumness – winner of Grufts 1980 – the Gremlin top Gremadog show.

GREMLINS THE WORLD OVER

We start this section on world Gremlins with the most successful Gremlin operating today— Sheik Gremashid-ibn-oil.

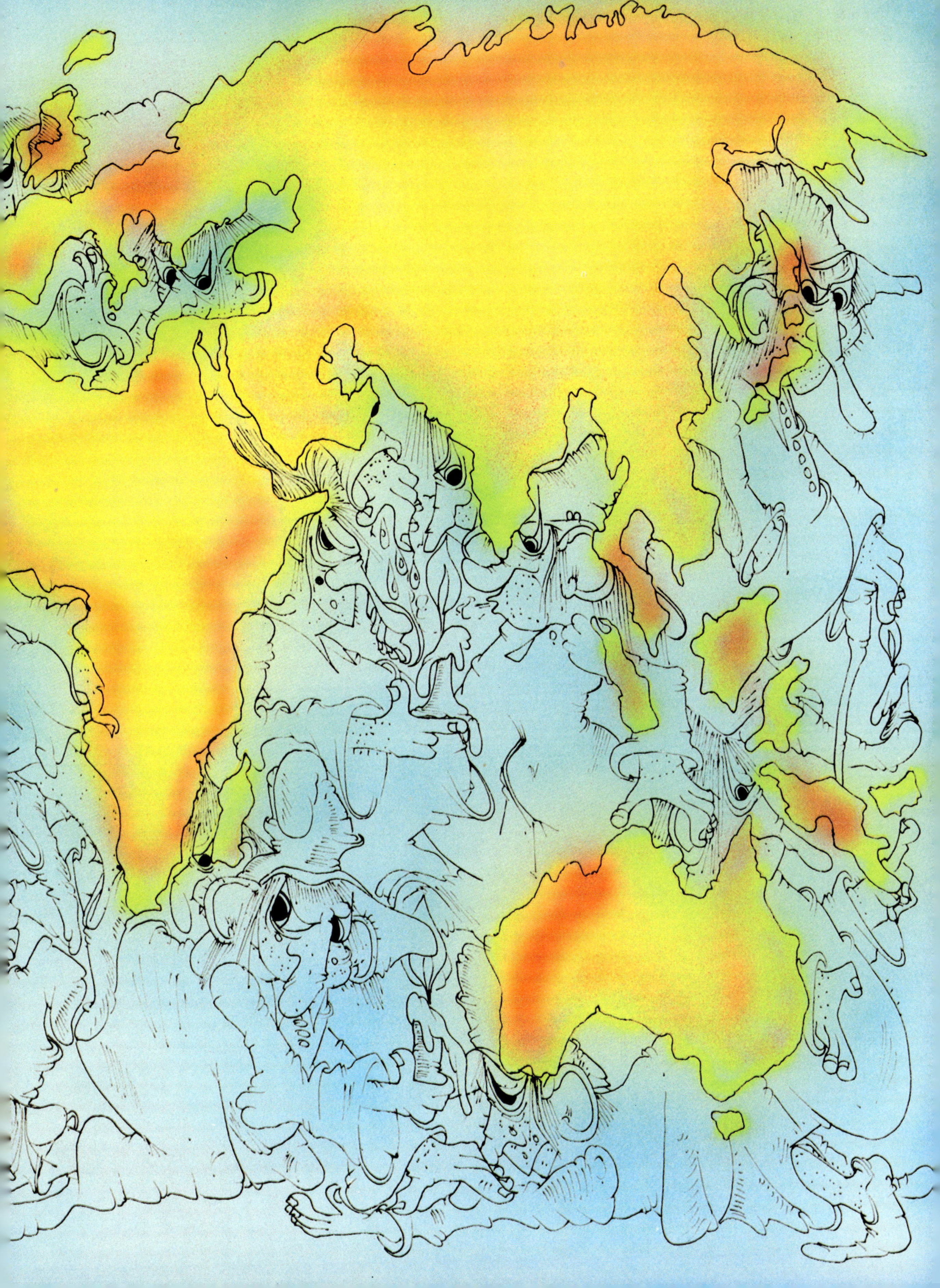

Sam (g1776)
and
John (g1066)
are always flying the flag in some way or other. Although Sam now has a bigger set-up than John, he only broke into the big-time a few hundred years ago when he organized a real hum-dinger of a tea party at Boston. Since then nothing has held him back.

John, on the other hand, is more conservative in outlook. His main interests at the moment are economics and industrial relations—two areas in which he is having tremendous success!

G 127
made his mark as
Baron Stroudel von Gremel
and became know in the First World War as the Red Gremlin, the dare-devil of the skies. He took more risks than other Gremlins in causing havoc to aircraft and pilots, including his own. Later, inflated by his success he took to the skies in the Gremplin, but this was a bit of a disaster. He now collaborates with Garlic, G 4711, who really knows his onions, operating within the E.E.G.-The European Economic Gremunity, inventing great grems like butter mountains.

This rare scene,
recorded on the Gremsel
Pass in Switzerland
shows Gremlins engaged in
their national sport,
of
alpinehornentrampolin.

G XVI
Gremeated ina Roman times hee tooka de nama of Disastrous. Sinca windinga upa de Empire he'sa changeda he'sa nama to Gremaldi- causa he'sa nota pasta it yet!

El Tauro iza lika red raga to a bull. He'sa always putting espana in de works.

Basel (one of the so-called gnomes of Zurich), although quite neutral, has an army of Gremlins working under him, specializing in time and money.

"O daffodil thou art so fair",
Cried Gouda with the plaited hair,
And though this maid was feeling cheesey
To grem a doff is not that easy.

Comrade Gremlins Nicolas-Rimsky and Andreievich-Korsakov enjoy Gremlenin things from different engles. They like Trotskying out new grems and have really made their marx in Russia. Infact their success has been quite revolutionary. In recognition of their services the centre of Soviet government is known as The Gremlin (the Russians have changed G to K), and prominent citizens are given such names as Gremyko.

The Mexican Gremlin Concarne is seen here recovering from a very strenuous grem. He wears a blanket, for although it is quite hot it is chilli to him. He has a girl-friend called Siesta and he likes to tequila feet.

Olrubbadingee withablee
is a specialist in grems
of the most primitive
kind. He is shown
here looking for
Roots.

The Eskimos of Gremland have an old saying. "Let everyone sweep away the snow from before his own door and not meddle with the frost on his neighbour's tiles, lest the Gremlins enter".

The North American Indians carved figures of Gremlins on tree trunks as totems of their esteem. The term "up the pole" originates from this practice.

Shown from top to bottom are:– Great-grem-hooked beak (with attributes candle and feather), Grem-giant-pink-ears, Grem-green-beak, and Grem-green face-crooked-hat (III), supported by half of Little-squash-head (Jnr.).

Grembuei of Gremanoch, a real clan-gar; shown here hanging on for dear life at the Gremlin Highland Games.

Johnny McWalker attending to his old bag-pipes— while his haggis at home.

Old
Chinese proverb say
"Gremlins once
released cannot be
captured by
the swiftest
steeds or
conquered by the mightiest
dragons".

Gremlins have been active in Japan for hundreds of years and have had a tremendous influence on the course of Japanese history.

Perhaps the greatest of all the arch-Gremlins was Yoritomo, a member of the Gremoto clan. He deposed the ruling Gremperor, a member of the Gremiwara family, and became Shogrem. Many of the grems of Japan are recorded in epic works like "The tale of Gremji" and "The heroic 47 Gremlins".

The Gremurai are perhaps the most famous heroic figures; they were generally in the service of a regional lord or Gremyo. A famous episode in their history is the legendary contest on a bridge between Gremisune and Gremku. Most Japanese Gremlins wear the gremono and follow the traditional martial arts of gremjitsu, gremarate and gremdo. Illustrated is the famous Gremurai Gremeyoshi cutting the flame, a difficult gremdo exercise, proving "Buddha cutting flame takes winking of eye, Gremlin cutting flame—many bandages".

The great Norse sagas of the Vikings and Viqueens (quite nice *boys*) record the exploits of Magnus Gremlinson (left), Grem Od (*nearly* left), Magnus Grem-foot (centre) and Gremfred Gremberg-Leaf-Gremlinson (tail end). *They* were responsible for spreading the Gremlaw and extracting Gremgeld. Their *voyages* even took them to North America – where *they* met the local Gremlins under Big Chief Terriblegrem. See also – Annales Regni Gremlinorum.

Bruce ere 'as no worries out in the outback, for 'is Shiela is apples and 'is grems are going fair dinkum. <u>They</u> get ya waltzing Matilda up yer billabong. The only thing 'e misses is 'is flake and greesers. Bruce's latest grem is a non-returnable boomerang.

Namastee – my name is Sri Mahatma Gremnath Gremiraj Gremgupta B.A. (appeared) M.A. (plucked) Ph.D. (by-passed), specialist in transcendental grems.
Oh my goodness, wat a luvlee tyme I am having making the grems in my native land – oh yes, I am menee tymes roping in my brothers, sisters, my sister's-husband's mother's second-cousin's brother-in-law and my country-men at large, to make such beuteful grems. I am always making my human colleagues get knotted – gee-ha!

Every four years, Gremlins of different nationalities meet with humans to do battle at the Olympic Games.

"The most important thing in the Olympic Games is not gremming but taking part. The essential thing in life is not winning but gremming well."

Baron Pierre de Courbertin?
French founder of the modern Olympic Games.

Gremapithecus
Australogremicus-
africanus
Grem-
janthropus

GREMLINS IN HISTORY

The evolution of Gremlins has followed closely the evolution of man. Although this follows Darwinian theory, it was not until the recent discoveries of traces of Gremo-habilis in Africa that any concrete evidence has been available. Naturally, as Gremlins do not die, the existence of these forms has only been discovered by a Leaky in Gremlin Control.

The earliest known painting of a Gremlin, found on the wall of a cave at Lascaux, France.
It is over 23,000 years old. Experts believe it to be the work of Cro-Magnon man, carried out while intoxicated by over-imbibing an unknown root juice.

GREMESIS
Chapter V

And it came to pass
that after the animals
had entered the ark
so entered the Gremlins,
male and female.
And the rain was upon
the earth forty days
and forty nights.
Fifteen cubits upward
did the waters prevail
and the mountains
were covered.

And when the waters
had subsided every
beast and Gremlin
went forth out
of the ark.

In 1932 an astonishing discovery was made by Sir Flinders Gremtree at Thebes. It was a papyrus scroll, which when deciphered proved to be the only surviving copy of the Egyptian Book of Gremlins.

In this section of the papyrus two Gremlins, Gremoses and Gremeses, are weighing their grems infront of the god Osiris.

This amazing text, written in the reign of Gremenhotep III shows that the High Priest could actually communicate with Gremlins due to the development of an archaic kind of gremelscope.

The Gremlin with the greatest weight of grems became Chief Gremlin of Upper and Lower Egypt.

Here is a perfect example of Gremlins actually helping human achievement.

After trying unsuccessfully for years to get their new invention, the square wheel, to work, Gremalith Gremlinstone played a grem on its inventors by using a micro-chip on the edges to make it round. Much to his and Messrs. Rolling and Stone's surprise it worked, rolling down hill destroying everything in its path. Thus the Council of Transport insisted that every wheel on the road be preceeded by a cart with a red flag. Hence the origin of the saying of putting the cart before the wheel.

An extract from "Gremlin of Troy"
(the face that launched a thousand ships – hence it was a bit battered)
published by G. R. Emlin and Co.

"'Heel boy, heel' – they shouted to Achilles, fighting like Hel en high water. He urged the Aga men on with a horse voice. 'Troy and Troy again', he shouted. He wished he was better informed, but it was a sign of The Times, so he took a day trip by Hectair to Paris.
Meanwhile the Trojans had a nagging feeling that all was not well, which was justified when the wooden horse disembowelled itself, destroying Troy with its entrails – then they all went Homer.
For my own part it was all Greek to me."

"All the world's a stage
And all the men, women and Gremlins
merely players.
They have their exits, entrances and grems
And one Gremlin in his time plays many parts."

As You Like It – or if you don't – blame Shakespeare.

The comedy and tragedy of the world was first acted out in the theatres of ancient Greece. With all those grems going on – they nearly come Acropolis.

Gremlinus Chaoticus Romanorum G MXVI
at the Gremetorial Games

Prof Posthumous,
a pioneer archaeogremologist
has translated a <u>recently</u> discovered missing book of Tacitus, which deals in detail with the <u>activity</u> of Roman Gremlins. Tacitus sums it up as follows—

While stand the Gremlins, Rome shall stand,
When fall the Gremlins, Rome shall fall,
And when Rome falls — the world!

— he was of course a trifle biased.

N.B. The Gremetorial Games were held a centipede (100 pedes to a centurian) down the <u>Gremlin Way</u>, or as the Romans called it, Via Gremlia or Vice Versa, depending on <u>where</u> you were.

THE GREMILOGUE:- Digitus plus? Digitus minus?

The reason why the famous sword Escalibur could not be pulled from the rock by anyone except King Arthur was that Sir Gremalot was pulling on the other end. When Arthur's turn came, he was having his tea-break.

Some Gremlins have a leaning for architecture that towers above all other interests – tilting buildings is a pis-a-pie.

Here we are privileged to witness Columbus on his way to discover America – courtesy of Gremlins. If we observe closely we will see the friendly little Gremlin oh-Buoy-(American saying), turning round the sign to the East Indies – after all, who wants to call the East Indies America?

Gremlins are *very* social creatures. They love parties, *especially* out of doors. Their last big barbecue ~ it was an all night affair ~ was held in 1666 in London. It....... er.... got a bit out of hand ~ to tell the truth ~ the sausages got a bit burned ~ and so did the *city*.... Come to think of it, the same thing happened in Rome in AD 64 when the Gremperor Nero held an *orgy* ~ but then he was *always* on the fiddle.

A famous scientist at work is always an awe inspiring sight. Here we see Isaac Newton, the apple of his mother's eye, escape injury as Gremlin Johnny Applethrower aims a pomme at him. Realizing the gravity of the situation he swore never to rest under an apple tree again.

Gremsie James
Gremeral Bustard
Gremonimo
Krematt Twerp

We owe a great deal to the famous Magniloquent Seven Gremlins, for were it not for them the West would still be quiet, peaceful and unspoilt, instead of being blessed with the fruits of modern civilization – only the Indians have their reservations.

"That's one small step for man,
one giant leap for Gremlins."
21st June 1969

GREMLIN PHILOSOPHY

After studying Gremlins for some time, it became clear to us that they have a philosophy on life similar in some respects to various oriental philosophies that have recently attracted world attention. It was only after we had the good fortune to come across Guru Ranji-grem, a mystic, philosopher and extremely learned Gremlin, that we have been able to verify our hypothesis.

For the technically minded, we should at this juncture point out that after initial tests with our gremelscope and having perfected vision, we added an audio attachment - the gremaphone, allowing us to both listen to and address Gremlins. Thus equipped, we have added greatly to our knowledge, and have had the honour of being awarded the Grembel Prize for services to the science of Gremlinology. But we digress. To return to Guru Ranji-grem - he confirmed that Gremlins adhere to the philosophy of Grem.

Many of the principles of Grem were developed by the Chinese as Chan and later by the Japanese and called Zen. Other elements of Grem are included in Tao and in some Western philosophies.

Gremlins believe in acting completely naturally - they do not try to do anything - but just do it. In their relationship with humans their intention is to act as an opposite force, the black of white, the wrong of right, or the right

of wrong. They are the mirror image — the negative of the positive and the positive of the negative. They are the Taoist Yin, the negative — or the Yang, the positive. They are the reaction to action.

Grem philosophy asserts that for there to be right there must be wrong, for sadness there must be happiness, for darkness, light — all of which they provide. They believe themselves to be the counterbalance of mankind, the impetus and restraint of human progress.

The reader may be interested to know that we have had to contend with Gremlin activity during the writing and production of this book. Although we have made contact with them we have had no special treatment! For errors, therefore, please do not blame us — blame the Gremlins — that way you will please them and relieve us.

We have been privileged to refer to the following works in the Gremlin National Library:—

Grem: A New Way of Thinking. Chang-Chung-grem.
Grem and the Art of Modern Waste Disposal. Grem-yu-pong.
Grem and the Art of Tri-cycle Maintenance. Treeweel Gremspoke.
The Grem is Silent. Gremute.
Compassionate Grem. D. T. Gremsuki.
The Dawn of Grem. Easter Gremfries.
Grem Bricks, Grem Stones. Gremonymous.
Grem and the Ways. Gremusai.
Tao te grem. Lao-grem.

How far that little candle throws its beams. So shines a good deed in a naughty world.

THE GREMLIN CODE

In the beginning, there was but one Gremlin. But as man was ambitious, frustrated and imaginative, other Gremlins were gremeated. Their numbers multiplied until they filled the entire world. Then the arch Gremlin, seeing undue chaos amongst Gremlins themselves spake unto them the following code, which they shall follow hence forth and for ever more.

No Gremlin shall covet another's grem.

Grem not unnecessarily - Save It - until such time as it has greatest effect.

Be ye always prepared to grem.

Gremlins ~ grem not one another.

Respect and honour thy neighbour's grem.

Gremlins ~ create not false grems.

Honour thy arch Gremlin who shall be selected from among thy ranks.

Obey thy arch-Gremlin in all matters.

Steal not thy neighbour's grem.

Gremlins ~ thou shalt have no other code but this.

Grem not mankind in hate ~ but in love for he is thy gremeator.

It is believed that this code was first formulated by Gremerabi of Gremylon in the year 2084 B.C.

GREMLIN
SOCIAL BEHAVIOUR

It may not be surprising to learn that some aspects of Gremlin behaviour are similar to human. This is due to their close association in domestic dwellings and commercial establishments.

The human habitat has now become so full of Gremlins that they are suffering severe overcrowding. Indeed some Gremlins have complained to us that on the whole humans do not provide enough places where a Gremlin can rest his weary head. And Gremlins do like their sleep. Although they do not eat or drink human food they do enjoy a good spirit — Gremlin spirit that is. This is drunk on all special occasions and gatherings such as weddings etc.

Recent world economic recession, perhaps due to over-successful grems has resulted in large-scale redundancies —

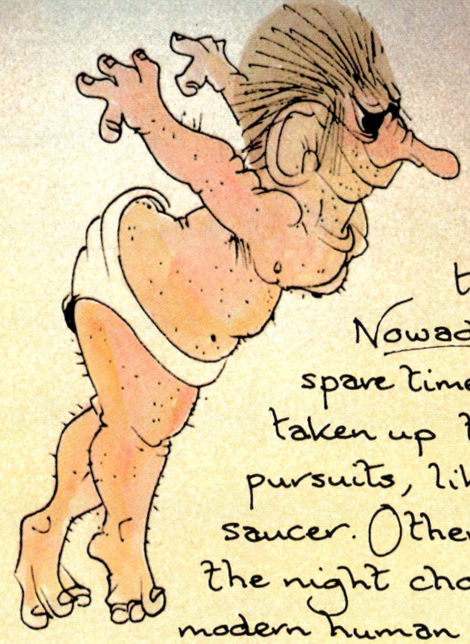

temporarily they hope.

Nowadays they have much more spare time on their hands, so many have taken up traditional sports and leisure pursuits, like mouse-racing, and grem-a-saucer. Others have found renewed interest in the night choir, while many like the somewhat modern human invention (in Gremlin years), the cinema, especially films shot in horror-scope — for they love the heroic characters which humans find terrifying. Others are addicted to hearing stories of Gremlore.

More aspects of their social behaviour will be apparent throughout the pages of this book. Their activities are quite simply divided between work and play, but whatever they are engaged in it always seems to cause some problems to humans.

We recognize the discipline of Social Gremopology is in its infancy and hope that in the not too distant future, there will be detailed studies of various aspects of Gremlin behaviour undertaken and published in the Proceedings of the International Institute of Social Gremopology. We are indebted to Dr. Sleepnow-Wakelater for his observations on Gremlin sleeping habits.

It will be seen from this
gremelscopic view of the interior
of a modern home that there is
chronic overcrowding. Infact
there isn't enough room to write
anything......

The ancient Gremlin sport of crashbangwallop has recently had a revival. Normally played in old houses, where there is lots of room, the game has today been adapted for use in modern, smaller houses. It is only played at night, by candle light and Gremlins usually have a smashing time. For some strange reason humans cannot pronounce the gremlinese and call it "bumps in the night". They don't derive the same pleasure from the game as Gremlins and get quite rattled, complaining that it is frightening and stops them sleeping. Not everyone likes gate crashers!

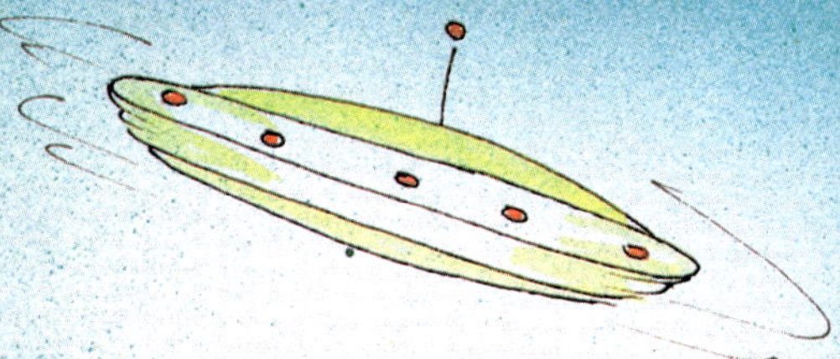

Gremlin Cratermass is the current champion of the popular outdoor sport of gremasaucer. The aim is to give humans close encounters or a star trek of 2001 nights. For some inexplicable reason humans call the saucers "UFO's" and get very excited when they see one. Even more ridiculous is that they actually think they come from another planet and are full of (wait for it) – little green men with funny hats and long noses!

They'll be seeing fairies next.

Gremlins love weddings, it gives them an excuse to grembibe the spirit of the occasion as well as to carry out a few communal grems. The wedding itself may be the result of a successful grem (about 8 months ago). Gremlin marriages take place at the same time as human hitches to take advantage of the facilities and festive mood.

An old Gremlin game known as mouseee
From Gremalot came to the housee
In dozens they ride
With a lance at their side
And dash to the pawn on the balance
For to pluck with a lance
Takes more than just chance
So up goes a cry "I'm a pawny" –
Which may seem to you rather corney
But it means that they've won
And have had such great fun .....
But all you'll have seen was the mousee

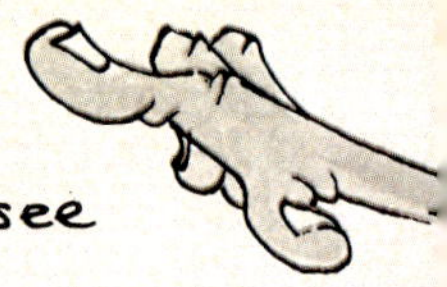

Sir Grem Betuwin

Gremlins love hearing stories of Gremlore (humans wrongly call them fairy tales). Here we see a group listening to Diedrich Knickerbocker's glorious tale, Rip Van Winkle. What is not revealed by the epic is that it is Gremlin Tic (the time expert) who is responsible for old Winkle's long sleep.

"My music is best understood by children and animals."
Stravinsky

Gremlins have such incredible voices, that they claim to put the nightingale to shame. Unfortunately, to ordinary mortals who can hear only the distorted notes of this dimension, they do indeed sound like the night gale – or cats.

"Gremlins and Gremlinas, we are gathered here today to share successful grems and to review their effect on humans. So let me ear your views. We Gremlins, such nice folk, have been largely mistoodunder. Why are we so baligned? Where would the world be outwith us? Nowhere, no how! We have, from time's first innings pushed men up the ladder of progress (not a pretty sight!). How would they have achieved anything if we, the Gremlins, did not make things go wrong? How? You and I know they would still be with their cousins in the trees if we, the Gremlins, had not helped them by putting obstetricles in their way.

It's oblivious to all what see the problem clearly that man cannot climb ladders if he has all the rungs, for he would have no incentive for ringing us up, no incidentive for improvement. And yet for millennia of services to mankind in every field (and hedgerow) he has not done nothing to reword us.

I ask you—if I caused you to sneeze on a banana skin, slip and boil on a wasting you'd been painting years on, wake you up in the night's piddle, scare you out of your wits with upparitions, or cause your bicycle to run out of fuel in a stormunder, miles from anywhere—what would you do? Thank me naturally, what else. What else? Fumans swear, curse, flame and peach each other—or just blame us! They are never frankful. What hazy features whomans are!"

Extract from Gremlin Gremaprop's speech at the International Convention of Gremlins. Los Angeles, June 1980.

Gremlinas, me dears, it's time we had a page in this book entirely to ourselves. Just take a look through the pages and see how many have Gremlinas – hardly any – what a cheek. All they want us for is our good looks, anyone can see that.

Even when we do appear, just take a look at the horrible grems we've got. Take a close look – cookgremming, baby-waking and the like. Anyone would think we were female! This is sex discrimination at its worst and what's more it's no good the author pleading that there are not many Gremlinas – we all know that – but he could have tried.

I blame that chauvinist of an artist, who's done all the illustrations, for discriminating against us – but then perhaps he can't capture our beauty. Call himself an artist – huh! Why couldn't they have got a nice lady artist – then things would have looked different – a book full of gorgeous Gremlinas.

But we'll get our own back. We'll take this book before the Gremlin Sex Disgremlination Board, on the grounds that there's just too many male references and all that sort of thing....... What about a Chief Gremlina? He could have drawn me as Chief Gremlina... ......or should it be Gremperson?

PUBLISHER'S NOTE:

This speech by the Gremperson of Gremlinas' Lib has been published here under threat of a gremming campaign against the book.

GREMLIN ORGANIZATION AND GOVERNMENT

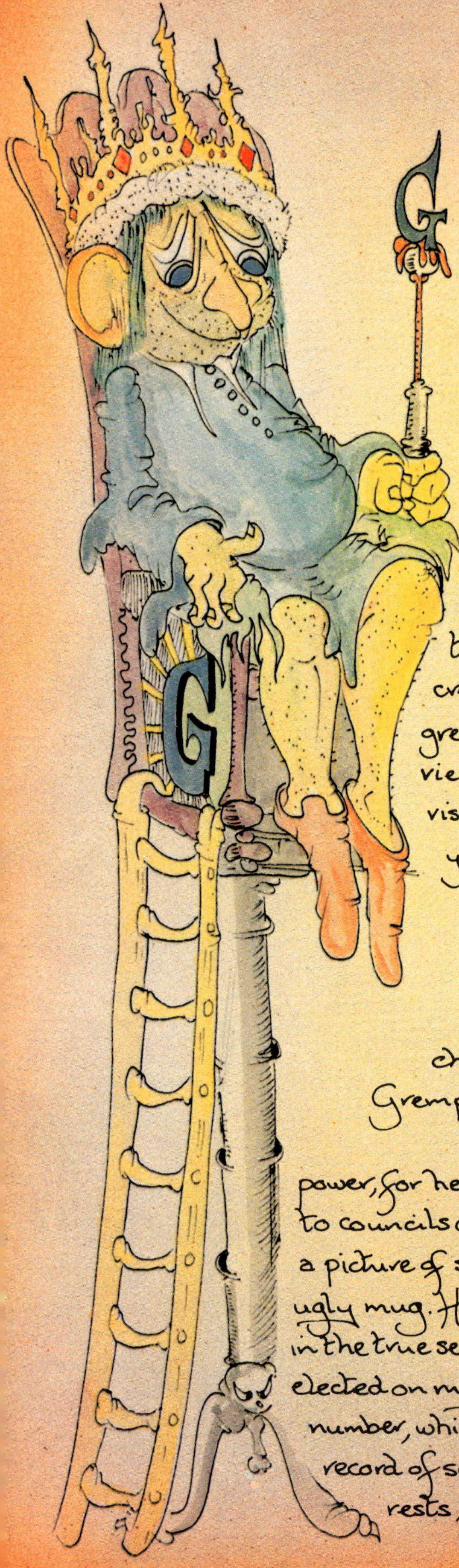

To the casual observer or to those unfortunate to be popular targets among Gremlins – the creatures appear to be completely anarchic – gremming at random. This, indeed, was our own view, prior to our quite unexpected and startling visit to Gremlin Control, which happened some two years ago, following up an unusually heavy concentration of Gremlins we had spotted on a field exercise.

Gremlins are, in fact, rigidly governed, if you can call it that, at all levels by a Lord high chief agitator – the Chief Gremlin – who rules his Grempire from Gremlin Control.

This inflated midget has complete and absolute power, for he is not answerable to an electorate or accountable to councils or committees. To mortals he is terrifying for he is a picture of success – the epitome of human ambition, a real ugly mug. He is, however, not a dic tator (an Irish detective?) in the true sense for his time is limited to a five year span, being elected on merit by the gremometer. Each Gremlin has a serial number, which is fed into the calculator, together with his record of successful grems. Once elected he normally rests for five years for he is an exhausted shell.

The runners up usually become regional top Gremlins, responsible to the Chief Gremlin, and do all the dirty work.

Gremlins are bound by a rigid hierarchy, which is reflected in the terms of address between each Gremlin. All grovel to the Chief Gremlin, who is addressed as Your Greminence Catastrophe and Regional Controllers as Your Calamitous. Gremlin protocol demands that on ceremonial occasions senior Gremlins, i.e. those with 1000 years service and over, are addressed as Your Aggravation.

We were sworn to secrecy not to reveal the whereabouts of Gremlin Control. It is a vast place, full of the wierdest instruments. In one section new grems are tested and in another new Gremlins receive their initial training, while older ones whose grems have become obsolete are retrained in new fields.

The most important area is Mission Control itself, (N.A.S.A. surplus) which we cannot show you for security reasons. From here the Chief Gremlin issues directives to Gremlins all over the world. The majority of instructions are, however, statements of wisdom like, "let them eat cake" or 'all humans look alike". A vast intellegence network, run by the G.K.B. under Paddy Grem McGinty (he's very thick with the Chief Gremlin), feeds information (the gremadog likes thick bits) into the centre, usually by way of Diameter (an ancient Greek Gremilina, the equivalent of Mata Hari). Mission Control has numerous gadgets such as gremex, micro-gremulators and gremputers and sophisticated equipment like pencils, paper and even filing cabinets.

On the rare occasion of a major international grem, the mission is planned directly by Mission Control and Gremlins are briefed (usually red and white spots with Y fronts) and are despatched after intensive training and checking of gremmunition. The missions are normally of a highly complex nature and are devised according to world needs.

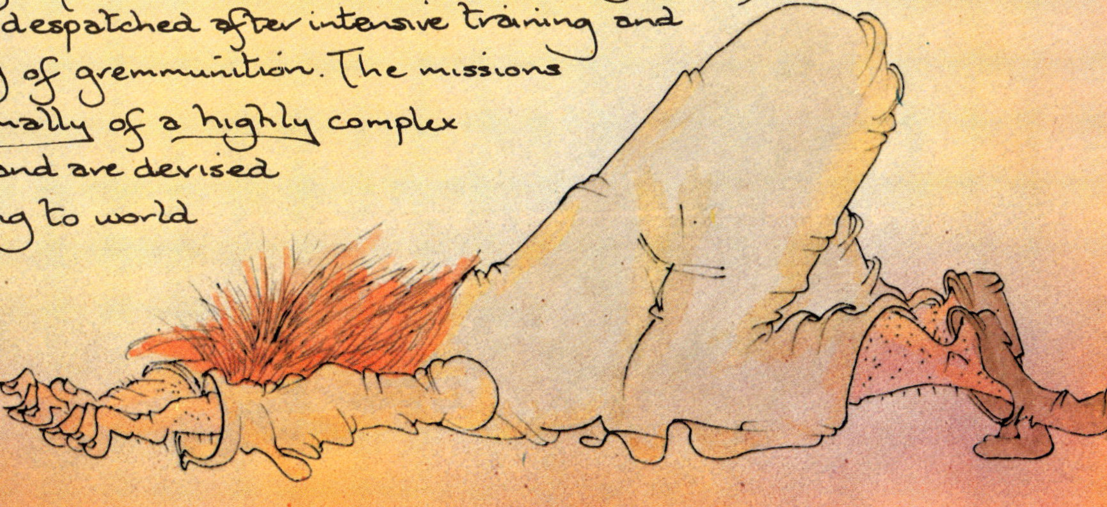

The open-air testing ground at Gremlin Control, used to test and develop new grems is very secret. It comes under the jurisdiction of the G.K.B. Here fiendish devices and tricks are perfected, prior to being used in the field. When special grems are required, they come under the top development unit of Prof. Gremstein. A special gremonstration was held to show us some of the grems they had under development—frightening! One or two were not shown as they had a grembargo on them, others were still in grembryonic form.

This illustration has been drawn from memory (as no paper, pencils or other recording devices were permitted), but is protected by The Gremlin Secrets Act 1927, Section V, Sub-Section 204, so erase from memory before turning page!

The official election portrait of His Greminence, most Catastrophic and Calamitous Sheik Gremashid Ibn-oil, in ceremonial robes, standing by the gremometer on the occasion of his election to the office of Chief Gremlin.

Three little Gremlins at school are we
We don't want to learn our ABC
We just want to learn to wick-ed be
Then we can have some fun.

But till we've passed our G.C.E.
(Gremlin Certificate of Education)
It's school as usual for us three
Then just as soon as we are free
It's look out here we come.

GREMLINS
RULE O.K?

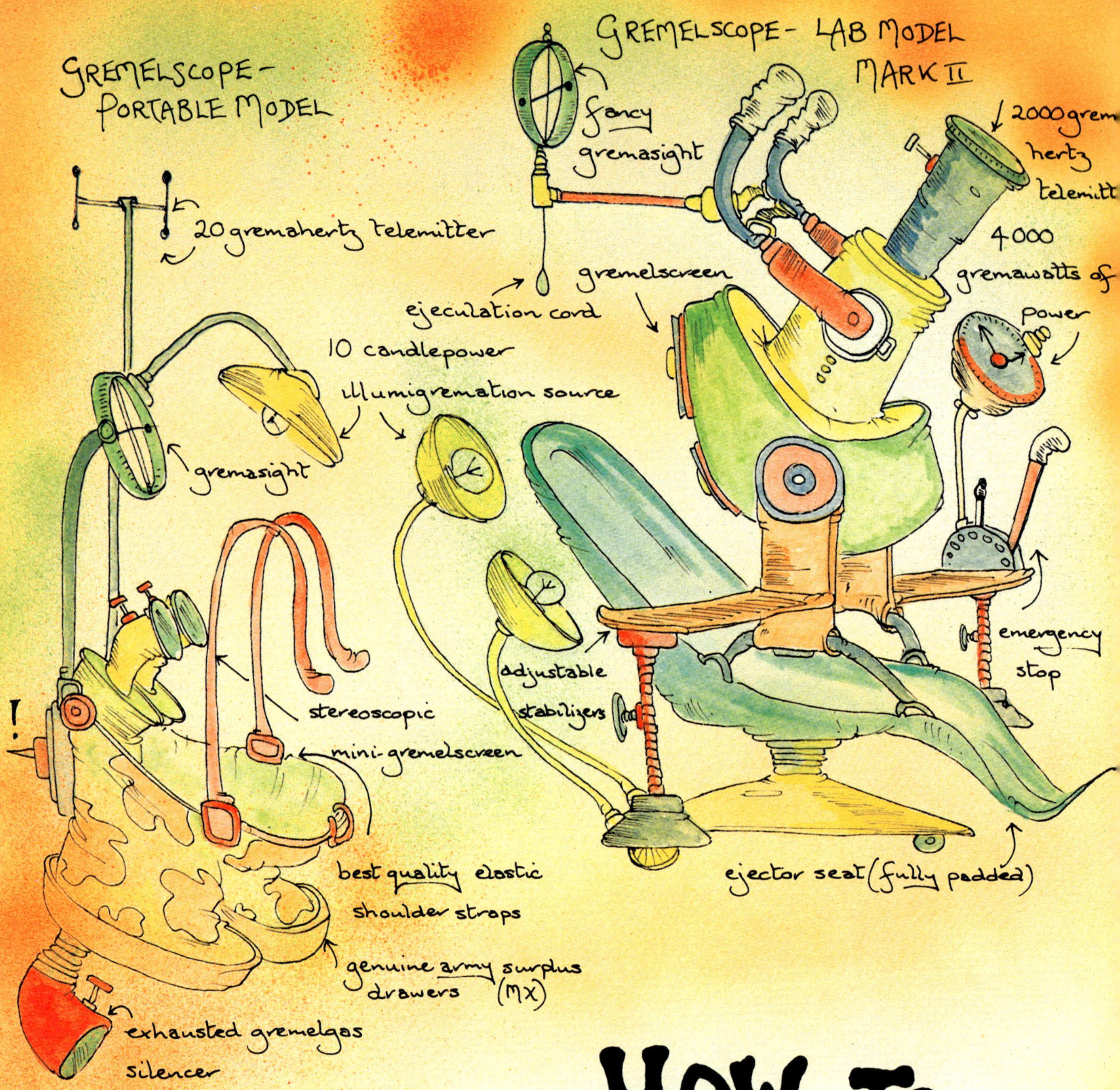

HOW TO RECOGNIZE A GREMLIN

In the course of the preceding chapters we have mentioned the gremelscope many times. It has played a major part in our research, for without it we would not have been able to see or communicate with Gremlins.

When we first started our research we knew from circumstantial evidence that Gremlins existed, but could only find occasional references in literature as to their form from the very rare sightings. In each case when a Gremlin had actually been seen, the observer had been under the influence of liquid, either alcoholic or non-alcoholic. It appeared that consumption of large amounts of liquid modifies the lenses and other mechanisms of the eye, and allows wave lengths which would otherwise be invisible, i.e. the Gremlins become visible. The ear is also affected so that inaudible sound waves become audible.

Having tried this out and found it successful, but extremely uncomfortable and unreliable (especially the morning after), we resolved to build an apparatus that would produce these changes artificially. This is the principle of our gremelscope – both the laboratory model and the portable machine.

Full technical details will be published in the Journal of the International Institute of Gremology (when the editor can be dried out) meanwhile the salient features are indicated in the illustration on the left.

Should the reader embark on his own programme of research, whether with the aid of the liquid approach or by building his own gremelscope, he may find intrusive elements other than Gremlins. It is always possible for a Gnome or Fairy to appear – but they are generally confined to their own books. Goblins, Elves and Pixies have also appeared, but none of these must be confused with Gremlins. They are a quite separate species of mythological creature – and not at all like our friends the Gremlins. In fact Gremlins do not get on well with these creatures at all, but regard them simply as figments of human imagination.

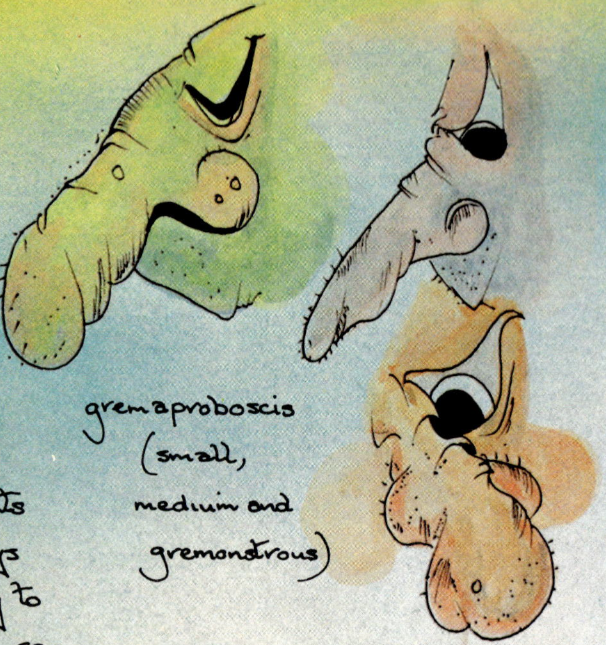

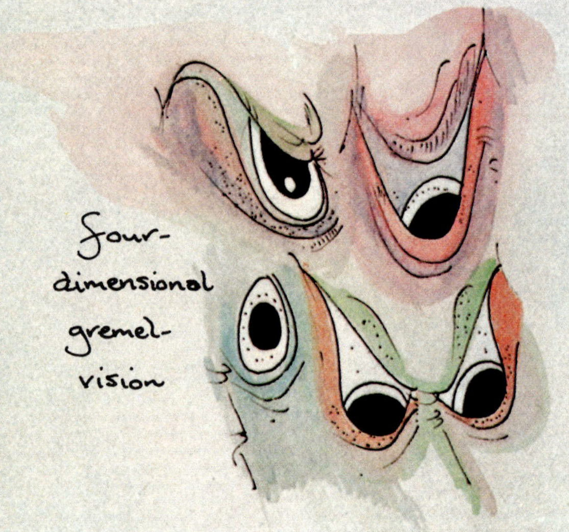

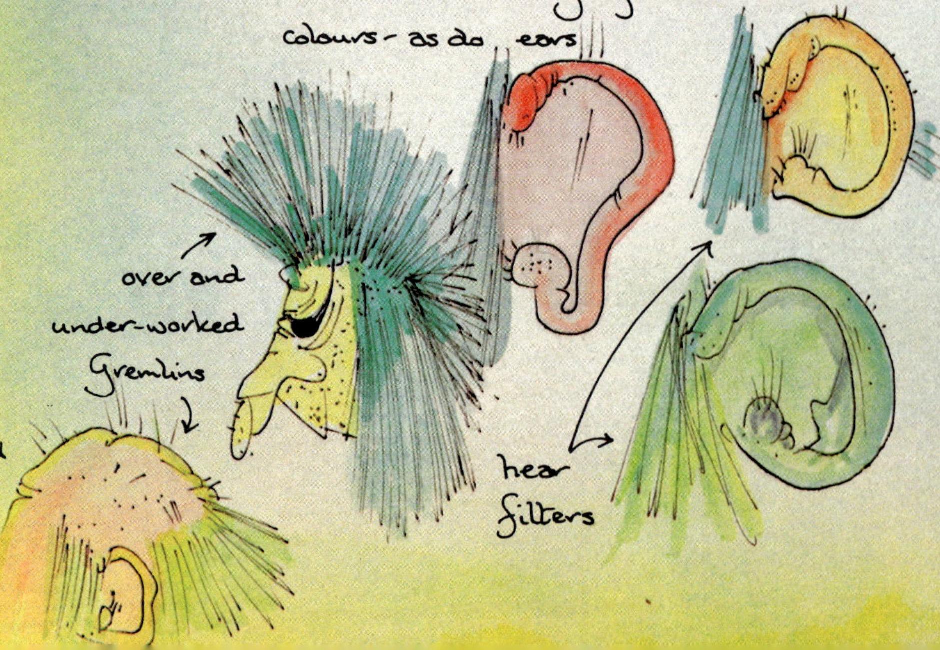

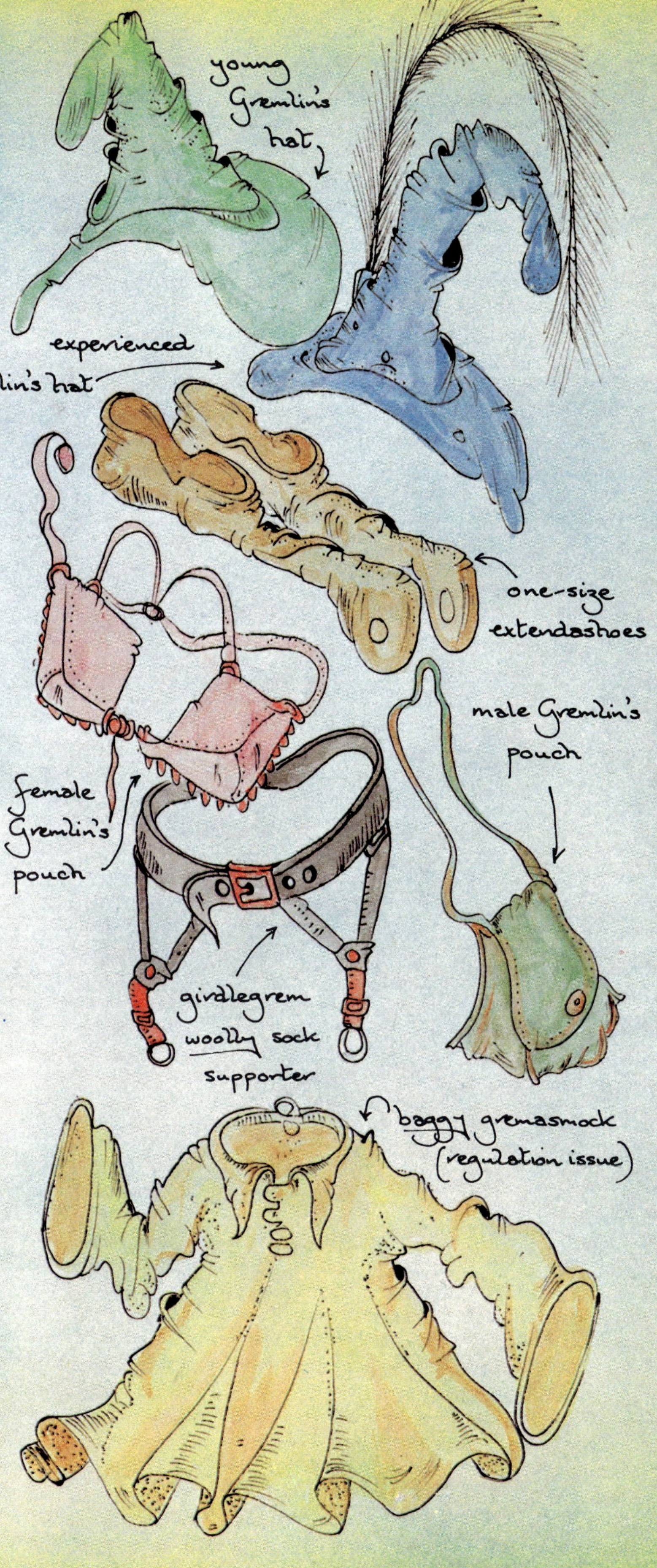

To help the observer we illustrate a few typical Gremlin anatomical details, together with common items of both male and female clothing and equipment. Those unable actually to see Gremlins may be fortunate enough to see evidence of Gremlin activity through their visual manifestations such as the Loch-Ness monster, the abominable snowman, ghosts, and other friendly creatures.

It is the red ey'd monster which doth mock
Ye visitors to the Loch
Is Nessie real – well, that's debatable
Or just a monstrous Gremlin
inflatable?

It's a big white sheet with holes for eyes
Through which the balanced Gremlin spies
And not the ghost of Uncle Hector
This strangely familiar green-haired spectre
For ghosts, spooks and other manifestations
Are only signs of gremlinizations.

Abominable foot prints fool high-minded explorers of snow-capped mountains. For these puzzling anthropoid trails are simply the work of their friends in high places — the Himalayan Gremlins. Although these mountaineers have seen the prints they have not seen the creature yet-i!

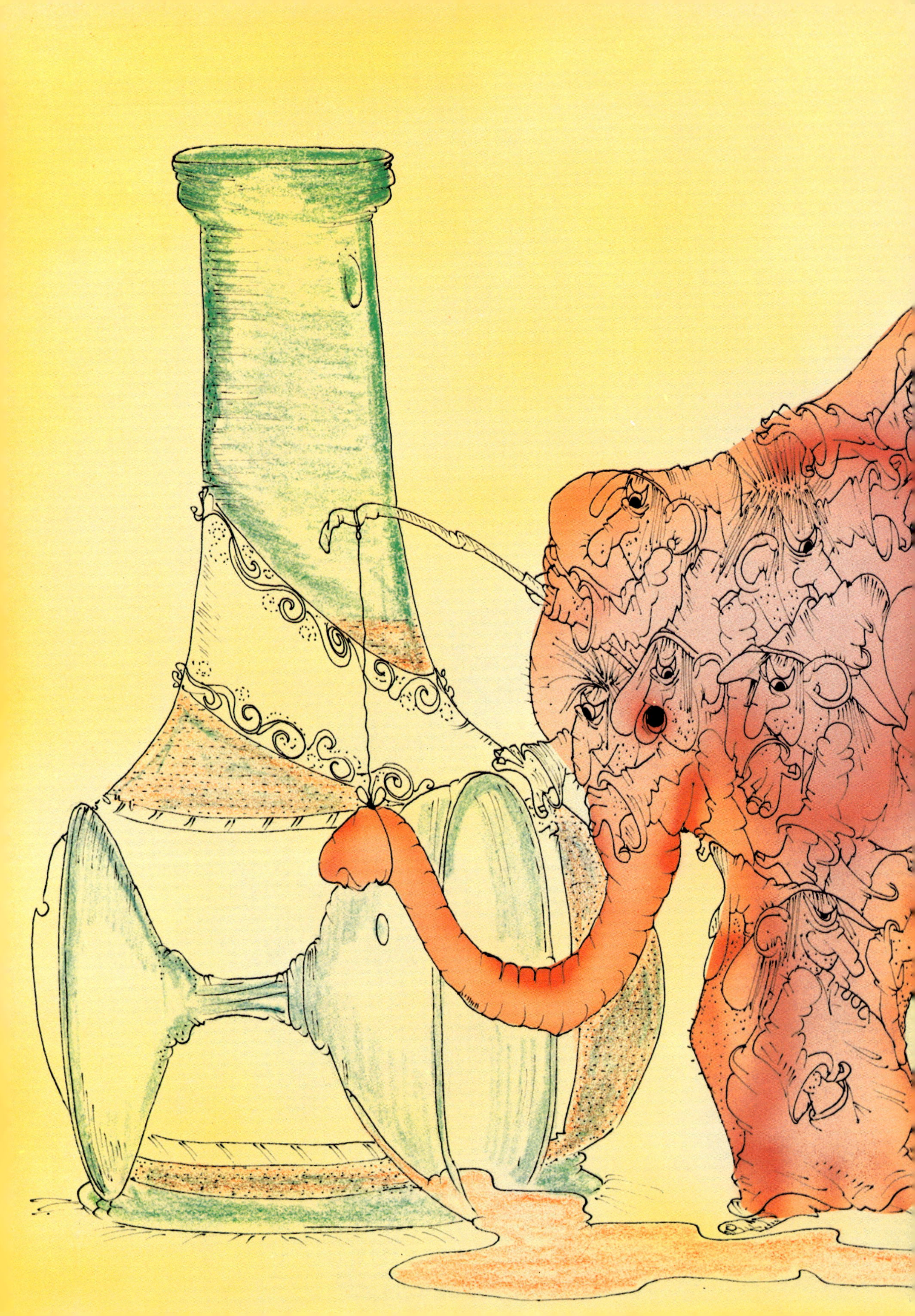

The only way to... hic.... shee a gremlin and... hic..... enjoy it ish to..... hic... dwinkee. Nelly here... this dear little pink pr... proboscis.... ish... ...a little embarrished about being.... hic... spread acrosh twoo pages but shee's having a ....hic... dwinkee with me......

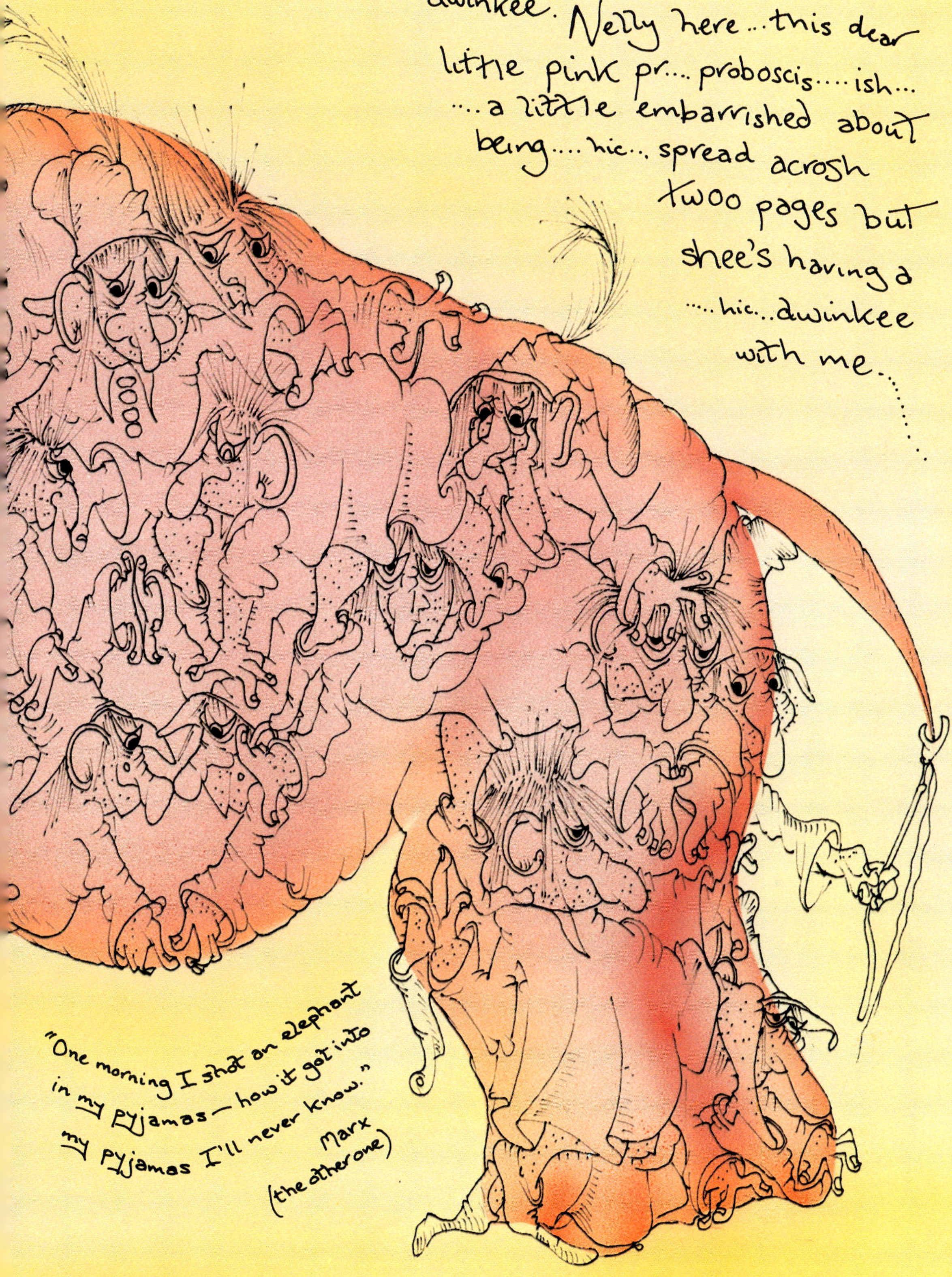

"One morning I shot an elephant in my pyjamas — how it got into my pyjamas I'll never know."
Marx
(the other one)

Perhaps the most spectacular sighting of Gremlins was that of a certain Mr Gulliver in the 18th century, who after being ship-wrecked and no doubt consuming a vast quantity of sea water, reported seeing scores of little people.

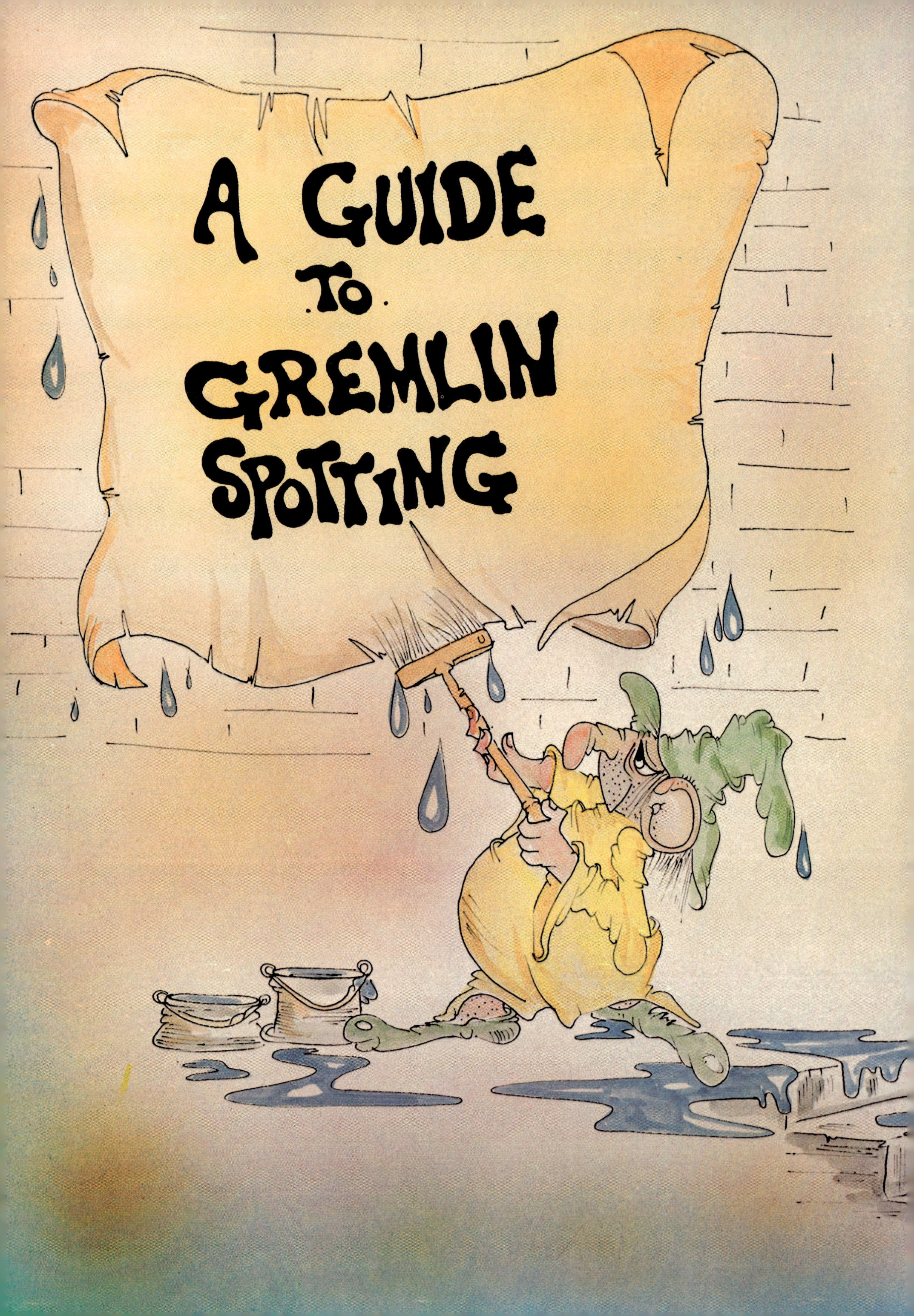
A GUIDE
TO
GREMLIN
SPOTTING

By now it will have become obvious that Gremlins attack all of mankinds' activities and they have done so almost from the beginning of time. We have also seen that Gremlins do not die, for when the job they were originally gremeated to grem is changed, modified or developed, they undergo re-training ready to meet the new situation. Thus, Gremlins have a vast store of knowledge and experience to call upon.

Gremlins are active in all walks of life and they are ready to engage humans in conflict anywhere and at any time. We have shown in the previous chapters, through the use of our gremelscope and specially developed techniques, something of their social behaviour, customs and philosophy, as well as how they are governed and organized. Nevertheless, the reader may be curious to ascertain which Gremlin in particular is responsible for his or her problem of the moment.

It is our intention in this section to present and describe some of the Gremlins that commonly attack mankind in his various activities, together with their grems, and include a few anecdotes and perhaps antidotes. The bulk of the results of our research on Gremlin activity is presented in this chapter. Most of our information has been obtained by prolonged observation in houses, offices, schools and factories in various parts of the world as well as from a detailed examination of all the fields of human activity that attract Gremlins. These range from work to leisure activities, especially sport.

In some cases a Gremlin may work in a number of fields, a Gremlin in this category is Tinkle, a specialist in telecommunications, who grems telephones in all situations.

On the whole, however,

Gremlins are specialists in their own fields, belonging to one of the following Gremguilds: The Guild of Household Gremlins; The Guild of Industrial and Commercial Gremlins; The Amalgamated Guild of Social, Leisure and Entertainment Gremlins; The Scientific Guild; The Guild of Transport and Ancillary Gremlins; The Guild of Political and Economic Gremlins.

The personnel in the Guild of Household Gremlins is most impressive. There are specialists that deal with everything from washing machines to toasters, vacuum cleaners and micro-wave ovens. Gremlins, like most other creatures, like their comfort, and the modern home provides everything they could possibly desire – comfort, warmth and work, for modern day humans have surrounded themselves with virtually hundreds of labour-saving devices, most of which, with a little help from the Gremlins will do exactly the opposite.

As well as the Gremlins that work in the house, there are also those that work on the structure, specializing in non-mechanical but vulnerable aspects such as roofs and plumbing. These Gremlins belong to the Guild of Industrial and Commercial Gremlins.

Also at work in the home are members of the Amalgamated Guild of Social, Leisure and Entertainment Gremlins. These Gremlins work in close association with

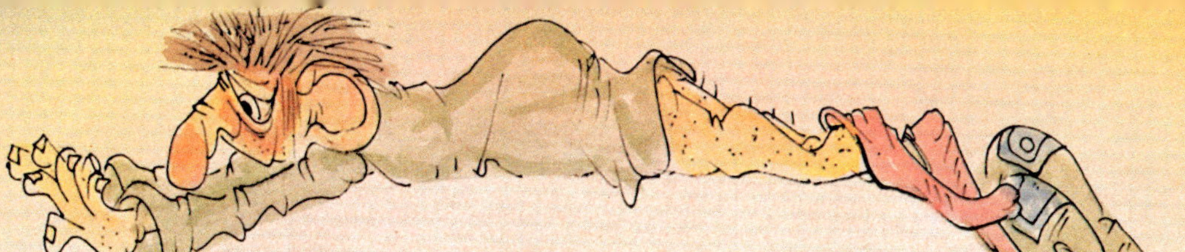

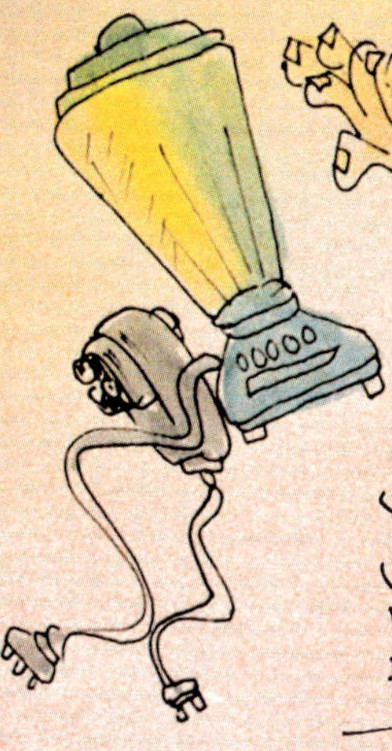

humans, many of them specializing in aggravating problems such as time (clocks, watches etc.) and with missing items. This latter group is responsible for practically everything that goes missing. The kitchen Gremlins are particularly numerous. They especially affect women, although they can attack men with equal success, especially when new gadgetry is involved.

The Guild of Industrial and Commercial Gremlins cover a multitude of sins, from typewriters and vending machines to major industrial problems. The Scientific Guild covers widely different areas, from weather to telephones, computers and electricity. Also covering a wide field is the Guild of Transport and Ancillary Gremlins, whose members are responsible for all transport and control systems such as traffic lights.

Membership of the Guild of Political and Economic Gremlins is by invitation only and includes specialists in inflation as well as civil Gremlins like translators etc.

There is no doubt, however, that the largest group is the Amalgamated Guild of Social Leisure and Entertainment Gremlins, for it includes amongst its members all personal and sporting Gremlins. They cover everything from embarrassing situations such as falling knickers to fluffs at sporting tournaments, lost money and ghosts.

You name it — and it's probably a A.G.S.L.E.G. member.

It has not been possible to include all Gremlins at work in the world today for obvious reasons. We have, however, tried to include a fairly representative collection – each is named and wherever possible his or her number given. They are not arranged according to guild or sphere of activity, but in the order we recorded them. Perusal of the following pages may, hopefully, identify the Gremlin you are seeking.

And now let us take a look at the marvellous world of Gremlins at work.

Opposite we see a member of G.I.S. (Gremlin Internal Security) servicing a washing machine.......

Det.(s)ergent Laundretti of the suden division, a plain clothes Gremlin, keeps a wash out for twisted knickers. Technicolly minded he mixes with scum, looking for leaks, but prefers it when the situation gets overheated leading to a general breakdown.

The twins,
938 and 939,
Splat and Splodge
work together
(when Splodge is not sleeping).
They just can't stand to see nice,
clean, laundry.
It makes them feel too conspicuous.

Fanny Beeton is such a culinary expert that she can even make a simple dish taste like nothing on earth – like moonrock for instance.
Some people seem more prone to her grems than others, but she is most active and successful when there is a party or special occasion, when she can always be relied upon to turn up a surprise. She is seen here preparing her new creation – Fried Egg Flambé.

G684, Sparky is a first-rate mechanic, some would say with a spark of genius. Engines are his first love and he always gives them a plug. Although he's been accused of being maladjusted, he has a feel for the internal combustion engine and can always gauge the situation. He is on top of the world when he's fouling plugs or altering their gaps, and has his own ring, which works only on engines. Novices work their way up, from nuts and bolts to oily contacts. For this purpose the modern Gremlin is equipped with safety clothing and miner's helmet, (Gremlin Safety Code, Section 49). Experienced Gremlins wear the traditional candle - it provides light and soot.

Gremlop 9520 x 13 is a tyresome, deflating little Gremlin. A great puncturer, he works mainly on the flat - but wherever he is you have to tread wearily. A member of the Transport Commission, he has quite radial views and goes into ruptures over successful blows.

Football is not the same in all countries. Mostly what people call football is played with the hands and what is played with the feet is fought with the fists and called soccer. At least that's how Gremlins see it.

These two Gremlin referees are always on the ball, preferring to grem off (both) sides, on the grounds that it's foul to all. Their goal is a free kick in the groin or shins. The Gremlin eleven may corner the majority of sporting grems. They've netted the Gremlin Cup and a Gremlympics Gold Medal.

To create inflation
is to inflate creation.
£
$
Lire
YEN
D.M.
Everything's rising,
Including gold bars,
Now we want someone to blame.
If it's not politicians
Then we think you'll agree
It's those dastardly Gremlins again.

It was tea-break in the office
There's no one to be seen
'Cause they've all rushed off—
coins in hand
To queue at the vending machine.

Back at their desks, all
eager to drink
Gremendous cries soon fill the
air.
I've got sugar in my soup!
I've got soup in my tea!
Then they know that the Gremlins
were there.

In recent years, tennis Gremlins have had to become very professional in their approach to the game, as some humans were actually making perfect serves! But thanks to Gremlin tenacity (and new trendy kit), Gremlins are again on top (of the net), and proving a danger even to champions. G 632, "B.B" is at the peak of his career. His best grems are "nets" and "faults", and he is at his most brilliant at the tensest moments of the top tournaments—a far cry from his humble beginnings as a ball-Gremlin, hiding loose balls, and making false calls.

To win, or not to win
– That is the question;
Whether 'tis nobler in
the mind to suffer
The slings and arrows
of the wheel of fortune,
Or to take arms against
a sea of Gremlins,
And by opposing
end them?
Shakespeare?
We need greater virtues
to sustain good fortune
than bad.
Duc de la
Rochefoucauld
1613–1680

You dirty rat – you shouldn't have drawn us on this page, 'cause we're the Gremanostra. If you've got a contract then come to us. We're the liquidation squad, experts in liquidizers. No kitchen is safe when we're around. We just blend into the background. By the way, so you'll remember us (we aint got no numbers) old four-eyes here is Baby Grem Face, hairy here's Valentine Gremday; with the hand-piece is Scarface Gremlini and I'm Grem Capone.

THE CHICAGO MOB

Mankind has been battling against Inundation, the rain Gremlin (g. 738), almost from the beginning of time. Over the centuries man has learnt a lot about his adversary and has developed elaborate rituals and formulas to do battle with or to overcome not only Inundation but other weather Gremlins.

One of the best-known rain making ceremonies is usually carried out by women. Specimens of clothing are first immersed in water containing a magical powder, swirled around and then immersed in pure water. After this the raiments are taken out into the open air – warm with the rays of the sun – and after offering them to the breeze they are affixed with a springy device to a line of cord suspended between two points! The celebrant then looks upwards, hurriedly mutters an incantation and departs. Sure enough, within a short time, the clouds darken and the rain Gremlin turns on the tap.

We are told that this ceremony, with minor variations, works in most parts of the world.

Gremlins have an ear for music. Whether light or classical, they're always around to lend a Handel.

Best known of the musical Gremlins are the Cacophony twins – Pianissimo Pizzicato and Sempre Legato. They are responsible for all the calamities and mishaps of stage or broadcast musical performances – including duff and dropped notes and mixed-up scores.

Here we see them conducting a gremonstrous performance of the Barbirolli of Seville's "Love of Sweet Orange Juice", in G major, with soloists Fortissimo Sforzando on diminuendo and Andante Previn on tremolanda.

Unfortunately the composer was always Chopin up his works, but now has gone Bach to his earlier style after a course of Beecham's. He was kicked in the Bartok by the critics for his first work for dustbin, waste disposal and drain – but after Borodin a new Boccherini he is now very Bizet. He says he will never Mendelssohn in other styles again.

In a camera with shutter open, quite passive, gremming, not thinking.

Grem Master Fuji Mi Nolta.

Talbot, a really foxy Gremlin, likes to work in camera. A world traveller and professional tourist, he visits exotic places as well as those resorts closer to home. His speciality is making sure the lens-cap is firmly in position when the photograph is being taken, as well as removing films altogether, so that the unsuspecting photographer clicks away in oblivion.

Familiar to all those in a hurry – the red light Gremlins.

The race is beginning
The favourite's on form
But there's one thing the punters can't spy
It's the anchor the Gremlins have tied to his tail
Now he's lost — but the bookies won't cry......

I sprang to the stirrup,
and Joris and he;
I galloped, Dirk galloped,
We galloped all three.

Robert Browning.

G.3455
Dan Druff

This irritating little fellow really gets in your hair. He strikes mainly at people with dark clothes. His aim is to introduce an element of uncertainty in those who, under normal circumstances, would be unbearably self-confident. A number of anti-G.3455 remedies are on the market – but for the best protection wear a "WE LOVE G.3455" badge – he's terribly vain!

G469, Sir Kit is a Gremlin of the old school. A few centuries ago he was principally engaged in causing breakdowns to wind and water powered installations. At the end of the 19th century, however, he was sent for re-training with special reference to the then new fangled electricity, so coming face to face with him became a shocking experience. He is gallant and chivalrous and when he arranges his favourite grem - a fuse blow - he does it with panache. A real gentleman.

Tic, G6.15, has made a life-long study of time. His best grem, which is simple but effective, is based on the alarm clock – a fiendish human invention.

He changes the time so that the alarm goes off hours before it is needed or – when he wants a doze himself – he simply switches off the alarm so that the unsuspecting victim sleeps on and on……

Oh young Lock-in-bar
Has come out in his vest
Through all the wide world
His grems are the best.

Securigrem Inc.

A large consortium of non-Union Chubby Gremlins, educated at Jale, that specialize in security. The only trouble is that their security means your lock-out. Their repertoire extends from simple household locks to new, complex electronic security devices. They also sometimes work the other way around – hence the occasional spectacular prison escape. They have a transport division, specializing in automobile doors and ignition keys.

Poker-faced Diamond Jim, G52, is a rum-hand at cards and an ace at most games, switching good hands for bad. He's never flushed with success and always grems to suit himself. He runs a club for Gremlins, but hasn't the heart to grem them. No joker — he always calls a spade a spade.

Gremsmanship – the art of winning by cheating.

"Height is no match for Gremlins."
Harlem Gremtrotters.

We have discovered that nearly every case of drought is caused by the over popularity of certain areas for Gremlin holidays. Gremlins love sunshine to the exclusion of all else – which is exactly what they do – exclude all else. Here we see the managers of the Grema-del-sol, Solar System and Solar Plexus.

Known in China as Ah Choo and in the West as Ebesneezer, G3981 is the arch enemy of anyone who does delicate work requiring the utmost concentration and dexterity. He always strikes at what humans regard as the worst possible moment, but which to an expert in the gentle art of sneezing would seem just the opposite.

He has a great sense of humour, often nose-tickling anyone at hand, just for fun. When on an important assignment, he normally wears hairy clothes and a feather in his hat. The tools of his trade are a nose-trumpet, tickling stick, pepper and sometimes Gremlin snuff.

His attacks can sometimes be prevented by .....a.... a a a h... choo...

Some enchanted evening,
You may smell a stranger,
You may smell a stranger — across a crowded room..........

Gremlins believe that all creatures should follow their natural instincts, which in the case of Gremlins is creating havoc and in the case of dogs, barking. To save hounds from slipping into dreamland, Gremlin Control created a special dog unit, headed by G815, code name Barker, who is qualified in pneumatics and is a fully trained dog psychologist. Barking is music to Gremlin ears and Barker is especially musical – his favourite composer is Offenbach.

Tap and Faucet are at the head of a multi-national plumbing company, with offices in the world's effluent capitals, such as Blocksville, Drainsburg and Dripp-on-Maine.
Tap is also well known as the author of "The Drains Came", — a Gremlin best smeller!

G.50 - G.100, a couple of mixed-up photographic Gremlins, do a little magazine work on the slide - although it's out of order - they like upsetting the show with upside-down and chaotic arrangements.

"She's just got baby off to sleep."
A spritely Gremlina said.
"And now she thinks that he's alright
She's going off to bed!
But we know different, don't we girls?"
She said with a glint in her eye —
"All that sleep's not good for her
So let's make baby cry!"

Oh, Knickers!

Waiter!
There's a Gremlin
in my soup!

UR

"The time has come," the Gremlins said,
"To go steal many things:
Like shoes — and socks — and razor blades —
And fountain pens — and pins —
Then hide them all where they will not —
Have sense to look for things."

Through the Gremelscope
Lewis Gremall.

G.32K
of G.B.M.

holds the micro-processorial chair in computer technology at the Gremlin Institute of Cybernetics. He was very Basic with only an occasional taste for chips, but now he is president of his data bank, with its retrieval system specializing in developing bad computer systems and programs and computer malfunctions. Smooth programs really bug him - after all micro-chips and computers are Gremlin assisted inventions.

All golfers will have felt at some time or other the presence of G. 12, Putt, at work on the green. A great player himself, he teaches proper respect for the game by making those easy ones miss, and those masterly strokes look like a novice making his first drive. A great sportsman, however, he also occasionally helps by arranging the odd birdie here and there.

The parking meter – that curse of every motorist – is in fact the greme de la greme of Gremlin engineering. It was invented and developed by the eccentric Professor Gremstein of Gremlin Developments, whose brief (yellow with pink spots) – (whatever turns you on!) was to create a machine that would regularly aggravate motorists and that could be placed in towns and cities the world over. These fiendish devices are programmed so that the timing mechanism is irregular allowing the meter to register a penalty without warning; to ignore coins fed in; to jam coins, etc. In order to keep them malfunctioning, they are serviced by Gremlina Wardens. Here we see Greeta, gleefully gremming.

Sniffles, the Gremlin who came in with a cold, is not to be sneezed at. His bell is a sinus that he carries cold and influenza grems in his pouches. When he plays his catarrh – which he keeps under his thick coat to keep out the cold – he sends a chill up your spine. Gremlins avoid him like the plague.

Television, especially when it's live, has been a growth industry for Gremlins. For it combines their love of intricate machinery and complex electronics with their sense of the dramatic. Suspense is the key word — will the film cut in on cue — will the teleprompter move — will it go forwards or backwards — will the cue-switch work — or the right film be shown — will the script be in order — will the microphones work or will the telelink break —?

If something goes wrong you can be sure it's the Gremlins at work.

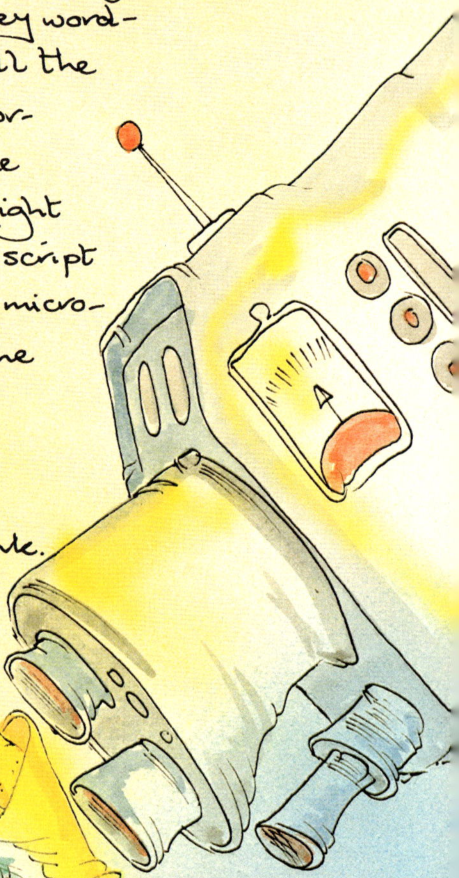

UNION DEMAND – More.

MANAGEMENT OFFER – 3% against a productivity deal of a 25% increase over and above 7% below the gross annual output of the world mini-eye-let industry's maximum gross profit, set against a re-alignment and re-grading of man-hour units, with parity for skilled workers engaged in the micro-brass -rivet industry, paid in stages across the board, over the next financial year – Gremlins permitting.

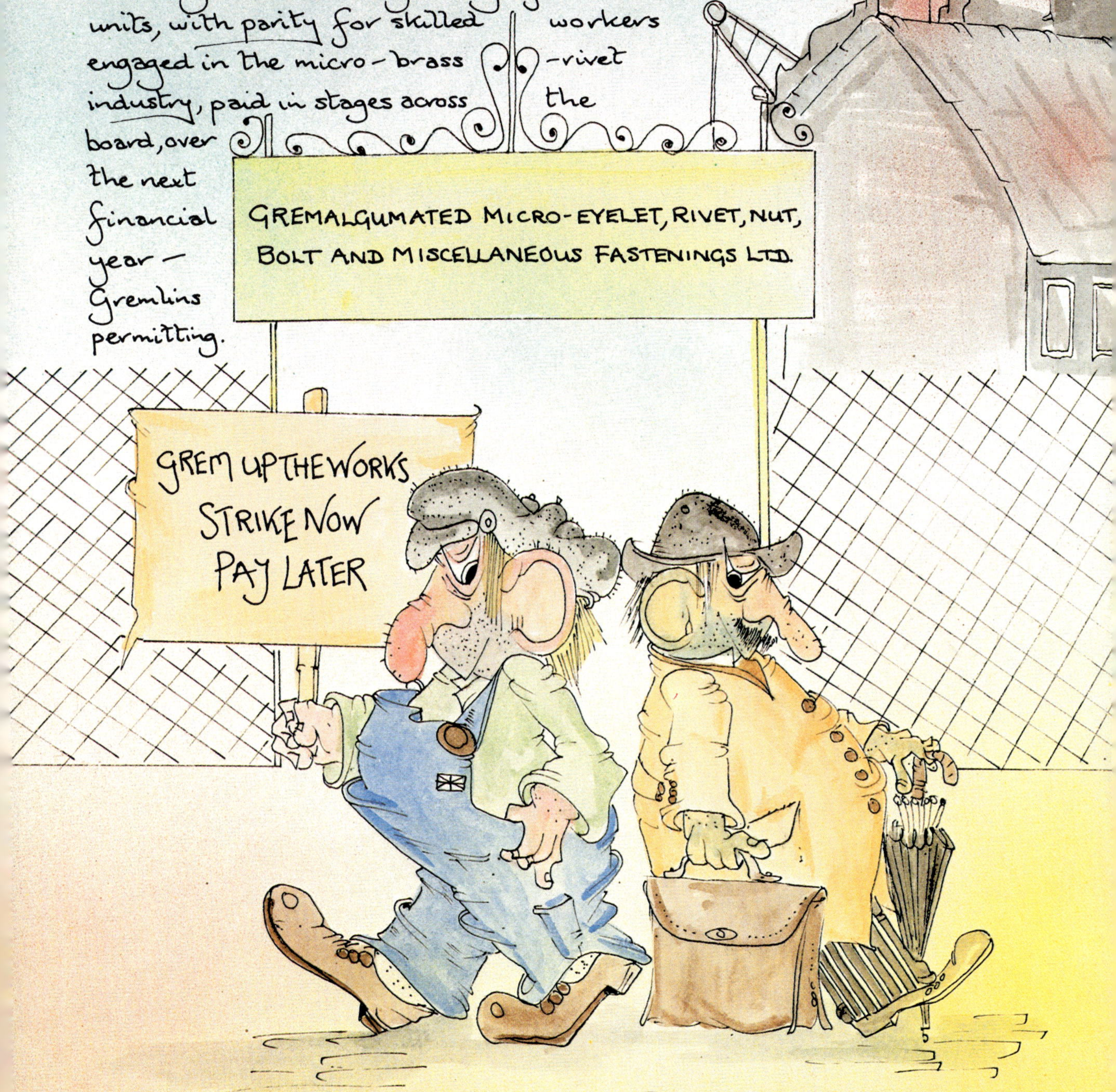

Joe Gremlin and Sir Richard Gremville are pillocks of industry, Samsonian pillars that is; between the two of them they guarantee to gum up any works.

CRICKET – A sport, at which the contenders drive a ball with sticks in opposition to each other.
Samuel Johnson, 1709.
and Gremlins stump the contenders with a sticky wicket.
Samuel Gremson, 1709.
(personal Gremlin to the above)

TEEPING RTEST

Tyhe th ick røund ox
p umps rover tghe hazy god

Hwt sick feown box
th umps mower the crazy b$_{o}$g

They [illegible] drown [illegible]
gr umps xxin the ..fog

hell - Gremlins !

The q uick brown fox j umps
over the lazy dog

How many Gremlins come to and fro,
In an English country garden?
I'll tell you now of some that I know,
And those I miss – you'll surely pardon.
Gremlins that can bring the frost –
Gremlins bearing slugs and wasps –
Gremlins that will cut your prize blooms —— – off!
There are holes made by feet –
And cabbages you can't eat –
In an English country garden.

Gremability Brown.

G.631,
the spelling Gremlin
opperates in all
languages. His work
can be seen in lettres, prints, manuscripts,
infact everiwhere the ritten word exhists.

Babel
is my title.
I translating all
languages as they is wrote and spoke.
For services you will thank me
from the heart of your bottom.
I am previously working at
League of Nations – now at U.N.

FOOT NOTE:

I speak Spanish to God; Italian to women,
French to men; and German to my horse. – Charles V, 1500-1558.

Anyone who uses a telephone will certainly have come across one of the most effective Gremlins at work today, G. 281, Tinkle. He specializes in telecommunications, both domestic and commercial, and has developed his skills to a high degree. He also has a rating for his work, which we can now reveal for the first time.

1 point — Telephone rings but stops before you answer it.

2 points — Dial a wrong number (when you know you dialled it correctly).

3 points — Consistently dial a wrong number – operator confirms both lines are O.K.

4 points — Introduce interference sporadically so that important parts of conversation are lost.

5 points — Constantly introduce an engaged signal when both parties are waiting to hear from each other.

6 points — Cut off in middle of an important conversation.

7 points — Crossed lines – this annoys two parties.

8 points — Co-operate with G. 815 to make dog run through room, catching phone and smashing it. Very effective! (regret dog not supplied).

An interesting note:

One of G. 281's ancestors once caused a major war between Rome and Egypt by switching the addresses on letters.

"We may say of angling as Dr Boteler said of strawberries, 'Doubtless God could have made a better berry, but doubtless God never did.'"

Izaak Walton,
1593-1683.

Here we see the adult G.380, whose infantile form was illustrated earlier in the book. An expert fisherman, he plays haddock with anglers, no matter how experienced, gremming them hook, line and sinker. Old boots, wheels and tin cans are often substituted for the one that got away.

Weather Gremlins belong to the Gremlin Meteorological Institute, an exclusive international club with members specializing in all conditions. Operating mainly from heights, they have been accused of having their heads in the clouds.

Here we see a gremlinstration of the expertise of the marbelous Hail ("Frosty-balls") Gremelstone (g.913) and Gusty Cy Clone (g.971). Hail says frostily that Cy really puts the wind up him, but he snows what he's doing. Needless to say they have a stormy relationship.

Oaths are but words –
and words but wind.
Samuel Butler, 1612-1680.

And now the time has come to say farewell to the Gremlins, but before ending they made us promise to reveal the truth about the greatest grem of all time. They told us they were particularly pleased, for it had fooled and worried generations of men – and had been the subject of numerous learned papers and books – as well as stupid ones – all of which amused the Gremlins greatly. For Stonehenge is nothing but a giant grem. Calendars and computers indeed! I ask you, would you build a calendar out of stone – or even a computer for that matter – have you ever tried? You wouldn't get it into your office let alone on your desk!

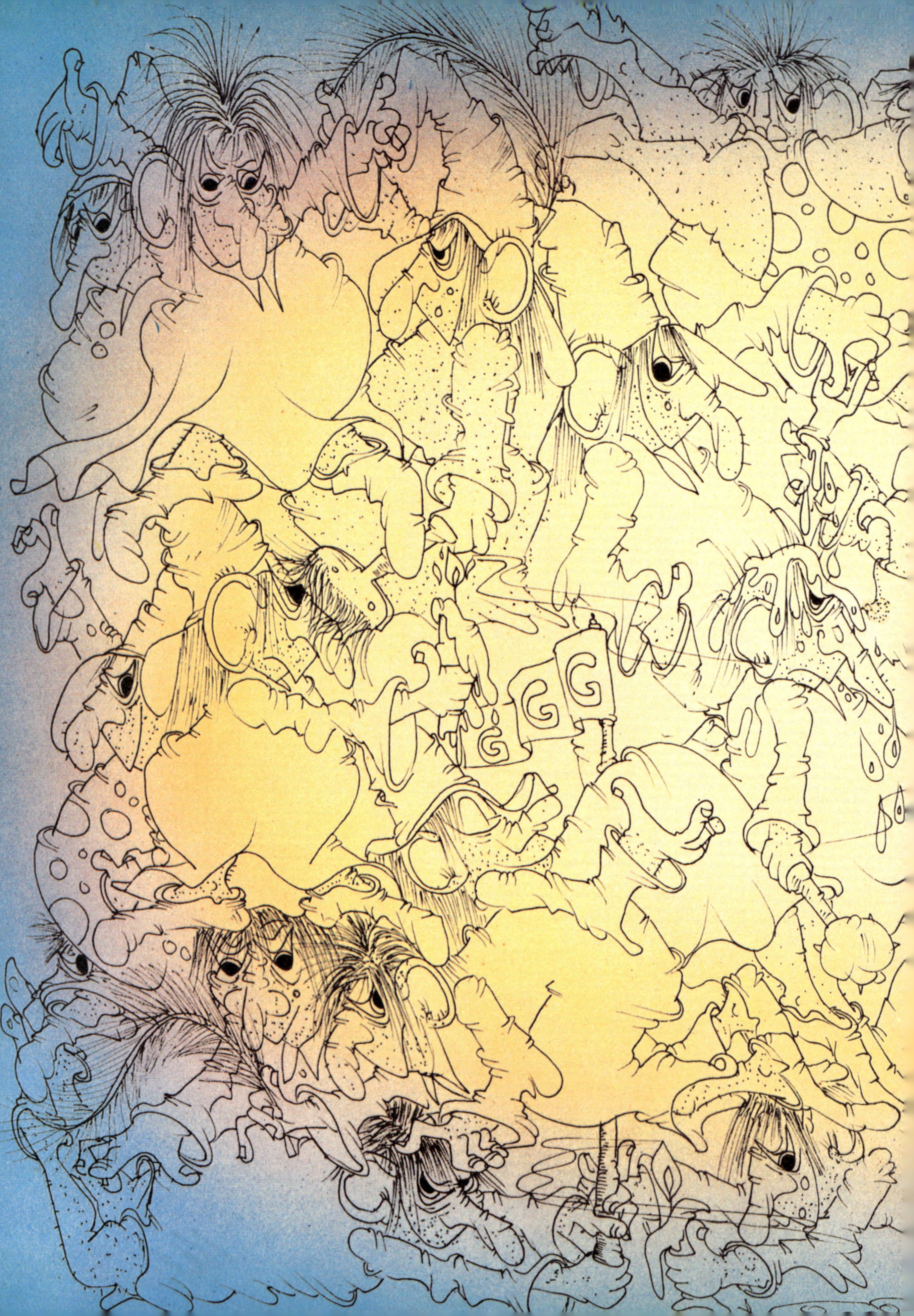
G G G